The Essential Work Skills Workbook

for Jobs, Community and Home

Self-Assessments, Exercises & Educational Handouts

Ester A. Leutenberg

John J. Liptak, EdD

Illustrated by
Amy L. Brodsky, LISW-S

Duluth, Minnesota

Whole Person Associates

101 West 2nd Street, Suite 203
Duluth, MN 55802

800-247-6789

Books@WholePerson.com
WholePerson.com

**The Essential Work Skills Workbook
for Jobs, Community and Home**
Self-Assessments, Exercises & Educational Handouts

Copyright ©2010 by Ester A. Leutenberg and John J. Liptak.
All rights reserved. Except for short excerpts for review purposes and materials in the assessment, journaling activities, and educational handouts sections, no part of this book may be reproduced or transmitted in any form by any means, electronic or mechanical, including photocopying without permission in writing from the publisher.

Printed in the United States of America

Editorial Director: Carlene Sippola
Art Director: Joy Morgan Dey

Library of Congress Control Number: 2009941903
ISBN: 978-1-57025-236-5

Using This Book *(For the professional)*

The need for educational reform and restructuring, to address the issue of the gap between the skill requirements for work and the skill levels of work applicants, are the topics of many management discussions. Business and industry representatives have expressed considerable dissatisfaction with the general level of preparedness of prospective workers. This lack of work skills is being addressed by both schools and work training agencies. Supervisors traditionally expect to train new workers in company-specific procedures and acquaint them with the corporate norms, standards and expectations of their workplace. They will also provide training in work-specific technical skills, but supervisors believe that prospective workers will have learned general work skills prior to applying.

- The excellence of your work will be a key contributor to your survival at work. "Excellence" is not simply a buzzword anymore, and most supervisors expect excellence as an essential quality for survival in the highly competitive world of work.

- People will be asked to perform more functions, be more productive and use more skills in the workplace. Because the global market is demanding more of companies and organizations, supervisors are expecting more of their workforce. Flexibility, a wide-range of work skills and self-management is the key to work success.

- Workers' "ladders," ways for people to move up in a company or organization, through promotions and pay raises, are becoming less hierarchical and more web-like. This forces workers to have a greater variety of skills and to be ready to use them.

- The need for training and retraining will increase. People lacking effective work skills will face being downsized in the changing workplace. Workers are being asked to continually review and revise their specific work skills.

- Corporate restructuring in response to the pressures of competition will create hardships for workers who are unprepared. Mergers, takeovers, and businesses closing will continue to be the business norm. Workers with the most effective work skills will be the most likely to retain their position and even thrive in the workplace.

These trends indicate that workers need to be more cognizant of the need to learn, update and utilize effective work skills. Given the rapid rate of change in the workplace, prospective workers need to develop new skill sets to cope and thrive in this changing economy. The spotlight is clearly on skills for successful work positions. Work is being defined by required skills and skill gaps rather than duties assigned to occupational titles. Though research indicates that work skills can be taught and learned, the purpose of this workbook is to provide workers and prospective workers with the requisite skills they will need to be successful in any work setting.

(Continued)

Adapted from *Lock, R.D. (2005). *Taking charge of your career direction*. Belmont, CA: Thomson Brooks/Cole.

Using This Book *(For the professional, continued)*

The Essential Work Skills Workbook for Jobs, Community and Home contains five separate sections to help participants learn more about themselves and the work skills that they possesses that are fundamental to their ability to work effectively. They will learn about the importance of these skills in the changing workplace and complete assessments and activities to define the required workplace skills and determine their skills gaps in the workplace.

SECTIONS OF THIS BOOK:

LEADERSHIP SKILLS SCALE helps individuals identify whether or not they have the requisite skills to be a good leader, and to help them develop effective leadership skills for the future.

WORK STRESS SCALE helps individuals identify how much stress they are currently experiencing at work and helps them reduce their stress by learning more effective ways for dealing with work-related stress.

CULTURAL COMPETENCIES SCALE helps individuals explore how effective they are in working with and communicating with diverse people in the workplace.

ORGANIZATIONAL STYLE SCALE helps individuals explore and understand their specific organizational style when managing their work in a work setting.

THE WORK-LEISURE BALANCE SCALE helps individuals explore how effective they are in balancing work, leisure, community and family activities.

These sections serve as avenues for self-reflection, as well as for group experiences revolving around identified topics of importance. Each assessment includes directions for easy administration, scoring and interpretation. Each section includes exploratory activities, reflective journaling activities and educational handouts to help participants discover their habitual effective and ineffective work skills and provides instruction for enhancing their most critical work-skill strengths and reducing their weaknesses.

The art of self-reflection goes back many centuries and is rooted in many of the world's greatest spiritual and philosophical traditions. Socrates, the ancient Greek philosopher, was known to walk the streets engaging the people he met in philosophical reflection and dialogue. He felt that this type of activity was so important in life that he went so far as to proclaim, "The unexamined life is not worth living!" The unexamined life is one in which the same routine is continually repeated without ever thinking about its meaning to one's life

(Continued)

Using This Book *(For the professional, continued)*

and how this life really could be lived. However, a structured reflection and examination of beliefs, assumptions, characteristics, and patterns can provide a better understanding, which can lead to a more satisfying life. A greater level of self-understanding about important life skills is often necessary to make positive, self-directed changes in the negative patterns that keep repeating. The assessments and exercises in this book can help promote this self-understanding. Through involvement in the in-depth activities, the participant claims ownership in the development of positive patterns.

Journaling is an extremely powerful tool for enhancing self-discovery, learning, transcending traditional problems, breaking ineffective life habits, and helping to heal from psychological traumas of the past. From a physical point of view, writing reduces stress and lowers muscle tension, blood pressure and heart rate levels. Psychologically, writing reduces sadness, depression and general anxiety, and leads to a greater level of life satisfaction and optimism. Behaviorally, writing leads to enhanced social skills, emotional intelligence and creativity. It also leads to improved writing skills which leads to more self-confidence in the workplace.

By combining reflective assessment and journaling, participants will be exposed to a powerful method of combining verbalizing and writing to reflect on and solve problems. Participants will become more aware of the strengths and weaknesses of their specific work skills. Inspirational quotes, facts and figures, as well as resources for further information are provided as an adjunct to the introspective activities.

Preparation for using the assessments and activities in this book is important. The authors suggest that prior to administering any of the assessments in this book, you complete them yourself. This will familiarize you with the format of the assessments, the scoring directions, the interpretation guides and the journaling activities. Although the assessments are designed to be self-administered, scored and interpreted, this familiarity will help prepare facilitators to answer questions about the assessments for participants.

Participants will be asked to respond based on their current work or any work situation from their past. Work can include any jobs they have had, contractual situations, work they did in the community, volunteer work, work at home, work with family or any other situation in which they were responsible for completing tasks. THE RESULTS WILL BE MOST EFFECTIVE IF THEY REFER TO THE SAME WORK SITUATION (PAST OR PRESENT) THROUGHOUT THE BOOK. On the first page of each scale they can identify the work they will be thinking about as they complete the scale.

The Assessments, Journaling Activities and Educational Handouts

The Assessments, Journaling Activities, and Educational Handouts in *The Essential Work Skills Workbook for Jobs, Community and Home* are reproducible and ready to be photocopied for participants' use. Assessments contained in this book focus on self-reported data and are similar to ones used by psychologists, counselors, therapists and career consultants. Accuracy and usefulness of the information provided is dependent on the truthful information that each participant provides through self-examination. By being honest, participants help themselves to learn about unproductive and ineffective patterns, and to uncover information that might be keeping them from being as happy and/or as successful as they might be.

An assessment instrument can provide participants with valuable information about themselves; however, it cannot measure or identify everything about them. The purposes of the assessments are not to pigeon-hole certain characteristics, but rather to allow participants to explore all of their characteristics. This book contains self-assessments, not tests. Tests measure knowledge or whether something is right or wrong. For the assessments in this book, there are no right or wrong answers. These assessments ask for personal opinions or attitudes about a topic of importance in the participant's career and life.

When administering assessments in this workbook, remember that the items are generically written so that they will be applicable to a wide variety of people but will not account for every possible variable for every person. The assessments are not specifically tailored to one person. Use them to help participants identify possible negative themes in their lives and find ways to break the hold of these patterns and their effects.

Advise the participants taking the assessments that they should not spend too much time trying to analyze the content of the questions; their initial response will most likely be true. Regardless of individual scores, encourage participants to talk about their findings and their feelings pertaining to what they have discovered about themselves. Talking about health, wellness, and overall well-being as it relates to work can enhance the life of participants. These wellness exercises can be used by group facilitators working with any populations who want to strengthen their overall wellness.

A particular score on any assessment does not guarantee a participant's level of work skills. Use discretion when using any of the information or feedback provided in this workbook. The use of these assessments should not be substituted for consultation and/or career planning with a career counseling/coaching professional.

Thanks to the following professionals whose input in this book has been so valuable!

Carol Butler, MS Ed, RN, C	Kathy Liptak, Ed.D.
Kathy Khalsa, MAJS, OTR/L	Eileen Regen, M.Ed., CJE
Jay Leutenberg	Lucy Ritzic, OTR/L

Layout of the Book

Materials in this book:

- **Assessment Instruments** – Self-assessment inventories with scoring directions and interpretation materials. Group facilitators can choose one or more of the activities relevant to their participants.
- **Activity Handouts** – Practical questions and activities that prompt self-reflection and promote self-understanding. These questions and activities foster introspection and promote pro-social behaviors.
- **Journaling Activities** – Self-exploration activities and journaling exercises specific to each assessment to enhance self-discovery, learning and healing.
- **Educational Handouts** – Handouts designed to enhance instruction can be used individually or in groups. They can be distributed, converted into masters for overheads or transparencies, or written down on a board and discussed.

Who should use this program?

This book has been designed as a practical tool for helping professional therapists, counselors, career counselors and coaches, psychologists, teachers, group leaders, etc. Depending on the role of the professional using *The Essential Work Skills Workbook for Jobs, Community and Home* and the specific group's needs, these sections can be used individually, combined, or implemented as part of an integrated curriculum for a more comprehensive approach.

Why use self-assessments?

Self-assessments are important in teaching various health and wellness skills. Participants will:

- Become aware of the primary motivators that guide behavior.
- Explore and learn to indentify potentially harmful situations.
- Explore the effects of messages received in childhood.
- Gain insight that will guide behavioral change.
- Focus thinking on behavioral goals for change.
- Uncover resources they possess that can help to cope with problems and difficulties.
- Explore personal characteristics without judgment.
- Develop full awareness of personal strengths and weaknesses.

Because the assessments are presented in a straightforward and easy-to-use format, individuals can self-administer, score, and interpret each assessment independently.

Introduction for the Participant

Work is of central importance in your overall career, volunteer or home satisfaction and general well-being. People who love the work they do, and who feel competent at their work, are more successful and satisfied than those who do not. You take a large part of your identification from the work you do and thus it forms a significant part of your self-concept. The problem is that many workplaces have changed and continue to do so. In this "new" workplace, it is important to develop the requisite work skills that supervisors expect from their workers.

While specific knowledge and technical skills gained from formal education, or at work training, have been necessary for people in the workplace, work-related or work skills are considered as important as technical expertise. Supervisors are requiring a much broader skill set from their workers, thus increasing the demand for more well-rounded workers. It is estimated that workers in the workforce will go from school to school from school to work, from work back to school and then from retraining back to the workplace in an ongoing cycle of trying to learn the necessary work skills required in most positions and demanded by the ever-changing requirements of the fast-moving workplace.

It is imperative to be responsible for managing your own skill development to keep up with the changes and new developments occurring in the workplace. The development of effective work skills in order to stay competitive is critical. Supervisors will expect you to be able to do your work, but they also expect you to be able to apply your knowledge of work skills. Adaptability will also be a key to your employment success.

Now that you know the importance of applicable skills in the workplace and you know you need to continue developing these important skills, the good news is that work skills can be taught, acquired, learned and practiced by anyone interested. You now need to be a self-manager of your own skill development and work development. Learning and practicing effective work skills does not stop with this book. You need to be a lifelong learner of skills, other than technical expertise, that will help you to be an effective worker regardless of the changes in society and the workplace.

This book, *The Essential Work Skills Workbook for Jobs, Community and Home*, is designed to help you learn more about yourself, identify your effective and ineffective work skills, and find better ways to use these newfound work skills to positively adapt to, and deal with, the unique challenges of the workplace today.

You will be asked to answer questions based on your current work or any work situation from your past. Work can include any jobs you have had, contractual situations, work you did in the community, volunteer work, work at home, work with your family or any other situation in which you were responsible for completing tasks. The results will be most effective if you refer to the same work situation throughout the book.

The Essential Work Skills Workbook
for Jobs, Community and Home

TABLE OF CONTENTS

Section I: Leadership Style Scale

Leadership Style Scale Directions........................ 15
Leadership Style Scale 16–18
Leadership Style Scale Scoring Directions 19
Leadership Style Scale Profile Interpretations........... 20–24

Exercises

Leadership Role Models............................... 25
Leadership Attributes............................. 26–29
The Leader in You 30–31

Journaling Activities

Future Leaderships 32

Educational Handouts

Situational Leadership 33
Leadership Quotes.................................. 34

Section II: Work Stress Scale

Work Stress Scale Directions 37
Work Stress Scale................................ 38–39
Work Stress Scale Scoring Directions 40
Work Stress Scale Profile Interpretation 40
Work Stress Scale I – Role Overload 41–42
Work Stress Scale II – Role Ambiguity.................. 43–44
Work Stress Scale III – Role Incompatablilty 45–47
Work Stress Scale IV – Role Conflict 48–49

Exercises

Stress Management in the Workplace 50–51

Journaling Activities

Work Stress 101...................................... 52
Stress Management 53

Educational Handouts

Warning Signs of Work Stress.......................... 54
Work Stress Statistics................................ 55

TABLE OF CONTENTS (continued)

Section III: Cultural Competency Scale

    Cultural Competency Scale Directions 59
    Cultural Competency Scale 60–61
    Cultural Competency Scale Scoring Directions 62
    Cultural Competency Scale Profile Interpretation. 62
    Cultural Competency Scale Profile Descriptions. 63

Exercises

    Valuing Diversity 64
    Interact with Diverse Individuals 65
    Understand Your Own Cultural Diversity 66
    Avoid Stereotyping 67
    My Stereotypes 68–69
    Respecting Differences 70
    Multicultural Collaboration 71–72
    Cross Cultural Communication 73

Journaling Activities

    What I Learned About Myself 74
    Cultural Competencies. 75
    My Cultural Experiences 76

Educational Handouts

    How Cultures Differ. 77

Section IV: Organizational Style Scale

    Organizational Style Scale Directions. 81
    Organizational Style Scale 82
    Organizational Style Scale Scoring Directions 83
    Organizational Style Scale Profile Interpretation 83

Exercises

    Imaginative Personality Style 84–85
    Rational Organizational Style 86–87
    Sensitive Organizational Style 88–89
    Structured Organizational Style 90–91
    Daily To-Do Lists 92

TABLE OF CONTENTS (continued)

Prioritizing a Weekly To-Do List 93
Priority List 94
Next Week's List 95

Journaling Activities

Organizational Style. 96
I Wish. 97

Educational Handouts

Organizing Tools 98
Interesting Organizational Statistics 99

Section V: Work-Leisure Balance Scale

Work-Leisure Balance Scale Directions 103
Work-Leisure Balance Scale 104–106
Work-Leisure Balance Scale Scoring Directions. 107
Work-Leisure Balance Scale Profile Interpretation. 108
Work-Leisure Balance Scale Descriptions 109
Profile Interpretations for Summary
    Work-Leisure Balance Scale. 110

Exercises

Work-Leisure Balance Scale Summary Profile Descriptions
Leisure Orientation 111
Leisure-Work Orientation 112
Balanced Orientation 113
Work-Leisure Orientation 114
Workaholic Orientation 115
Balancing Work and Leisure. 116–117

Journaling Activities

Workaholism or Not. 118
My Work. 119

Educational Handouts

Finding Your Balance Between Work and Leisure. 120
Why Leisure Matters. 121

SECTION I:
Leadership Style Scale

NAME _____ DATE _____

Before completing these scales, decide whether you want to respond to the scale based on your *current* work situation or one you had in the *past*. The work can be a job, a part-time job, volunteer work in your community, work at home, work with your family, a contractual situation or any other time where you are responsible for completing certain tasks. Write that work below. Refer to this work throughout these scales.

WORK _____

Leadership Style Scale Directions

Most people are leaders or potential leaders. If you lead people at home, at work, or in your community, you have a specific leadership style that allows you to accomplish tasks at hand. It is important to identify the style you use in leading others. Similarly, if you are an aspiring leader, learning more about your leadership style, along with the strengths and weaknesses associated with that style, is important in your success.

Leadership style is the manner and approach you use in providing direction to other people, implementing plans that have been developed and motivating people to complete tasks. The Leadership Style Scale can help you identify the approach that you use in leading other people.

This scale contains 50 statements divided into five leadership styles. Read each statement and decide the extent to which the statement best describes you.

In the following example, the circled 2 indicates that the item is Somewhat Descriptive for the person completing the scale:

3 = Very Descriptive   **2 = Somewhat Descriptive**   **1 = Not Very Descriptive**

When leading a group of people, I . . .

1. encourage them to make all decisions independently   3   (2)   1

This is not a test and there are no right or wrong answers. Do not spend too much time thinking about your answers. Your initial response will likely be the most true for you. Be sure to respond to every statement.

(Turn to the next page and begin)

SECTION I: LEADERSHIP STYLE SCALE

Leadership Style Scale

3 = Very Descriptive   **2 = Somewhat Descriptive**   **1 = Not Very Descriptive**

When leading a group of people, I . . .

1. encourage them to make all decisions independently	3	2	1
2. expect them do things because I say so	3	2	1
3. give clear directions in times of emergencies	3	2	1
4. provide clear expectations about what must be done	3	2	1
5. enjoy telling people what to do	3	2	1
6. like to tell them what needs to be done	3	2	1
7. want them to follow directions exactly	3	2	1
8. do not rely on input from them	3	2	1
9. do not trust them to do things	3	2	1
10. always proceed "by the book"	3	2	1

Style 1 Total _____

When leading a group of people, I . . .

11. appreciate feedback from them	3	2	1
12. love just being with them	3	2	1
13. want them to feel in control of their destiny	3	2	1
14. listen to concerns or suggestions	3	2	1
15. believe that they are as important as the completion of the task	3	2	1
16. like to offer guidance to them	3	2	1
17. always try to build personal relationships	3	2	1
18. like them to help me with decision making	3	2	1
19. allow them to help in establishing goals	3	2	1
20. work side by side with them to get the task done	3	2	1

Style 2 Total _____

(Continued on the next page)

SECTION I: LEADERSHIP STYLE SCALE

(Leadership Style Scale *continued*)

| | 3 = Very Descriptive | 2 = Somewhat Descriptive | 1 = Not Very Descriptive |

When leading a group of people, I . . .

21. leave them alone to do their work	3	2	1
22. give them as much freedom as possible	3	2	1
23. delegate tasks to them as needed	3	2	1
24. let them determine the project's direction	3	2	1
25. allow them to make their own decisions	3	2	1
26. offer as little guidance as possible	3	2	1
27. use a "hands off" approach to get things done	3	2	1
28. like to give authority to them	3	2	1
29. believe that they need to take ownership of tasks	3	2	1
30. monitor what is going on and step in only if I need to	3	2	1

Style 3 Total _____

When leading a group of people, I . . .

31. act as charming or charismatic as possible	3	2	1
32. motivate them easily and quickly	3	2	1
33. inspire them with my vision of the task	3	2	1
34. delegate responsibility to them, then mentor them	3	2	1
35. show as much enthusiasm for the task as possible	3	2	1
36. drive people to perform through my energy	3	2	1
37. like to discuss how their efforts will contribute	3	2	1
38. like to share power with them	3	2	1
39. like to spend a lot of time communicating with them	3	2	1
40. work to pick up on their moods and concerns	3	2	1

Style 4 Total _____

(Continued on the next page)

SECTION I: LEADERSHIP STYLE SCALE

(Leadership Style Scale continued)

	3 = Very Descriptive	2 = Somewhat Descriptive	1 = Not Very Descriptive

When leading a group of people, I . . .

41. give them praise as much as possible	3	2	1
42. provide a lot of positive feedback	3	2	1
43. create an environment where people feel appreciated	3	2	1
44. trust them to make their own decisions	3	2	1
45. recognize their participation as well as results	3	2	1
46. listen actively to what they say	3	2	1
47. stand up for them when I need to	3	2	1
48. model behaviors I want them to exhibit	3	2	1
49. recognize their contributions in public	3	2	1
50. keep them informed of new developments in the task	3	2	1

Style 5 Total _____

(Go to the Scoring Directions on the next page)

SECTION I: LEADERSHIP STYLE SCALE

Leadership Style Scale
Scoring Directions

This scale is designed to help you to identify the specific style you use when you are leading other people. To score the scale, you need to determine your scores on each of the individual scales and identify your highest score. People use five primary styles when leading and the five sections on the scale reflect these:

>Authoritarian Style
>
>Democratic Style
>
>Hands-off Style
>
>Charismatic Style
>
>Motivational Style

To score the scale:

For each section, count the scores you circled for each of the five sections. Write that total on the line marked "Total" at the end of the section. Then, transfer your totals to the spaces below:

>Style 1 (Authoritarian Style) = _____
>
>Style 2 (Democratic Style) = _____
>
>Style 3 (Hands-off Style) = _____
>
>Style 4 (Charismatic Style) = _____
>
>Style 5 (Motivational Style) = _____

To be effective in providing leadership for other people, you probably use all five of the styles. The area (or areas) in which you scored the highest tends to be your most preferred leadership style(s). Similarly, the area or areas in which you scored the lowest tends to be your least preferred leadership style(s). Now turn to the next page for a description of each of the five scales on the assessment.

SECTION I: LEADERSHIP STYLE SCALE

Profile Interpretation
Authoritarian Style

In this leadership style, the leader exerts high levels of power over his or her employees or team members. When using this leadership style, you are reluctant to accept suggestions from your team members.

If the Authoritarian Style is your leadership style . . .

List times when this leadership style has worked well for you.

_____

_____

_____

_____

List times when this leadership style has not worked well for you.

_____

_____

_____

_____

Compare and contrast situations in which this style has and has not worked well. What do you notice?

_____

_____

_____

_____

(Continued on the next page)

SECTION I: LEADERSHIP STYLE SCALE

Profile Interpretation
Democratic Style

In this leadership style, the leader will make most final decisions. However, he or she invites other team members to contribute to the decision-making process. The leader tries to ensure that team members have some control over their own destiny.

If the Democratic Style is your leadership style . . .

List times when this leadership style has worked well for you.

_____

_____

_____

_____

List times when this leadership style has not worked well for you.

_____

_____

_____

_____

Compare and contrast situations in which this style has and has not worked well. What do you notice?

_____

_____

_____

_____

(Continued on the next page)

SECTION I: LEADERSHIP STYLE SCALE

Profile Interpretation
Hands-Off Style

In this leadership style, the leader takes a hands-off approach to team decision making. This leader trusts that team members are capable of doing their tasks with limited supervision. The leader will monitor what is being achieved and communicates this back to the team.

If the Hands-Off Style is your leadership style . . .

List times when this leadership style has worked well for you.

_____

_____

_____

_____

List times when this leadership style has not worked well for you.

_____

_____

_____

_____

Compare and contrast situations in which this style has and has not worked well. What do you notice?

_____

_____

_____

_____

(Continued on the next page)

SECTION I: LEADERSHIP STYLE SCALE

Profile Interpretation
Charismatic Style

In this leadership style, the leader inspires his or her team members with a shared vision of the final goal to be achieved. This leader is highly visible and believes that communication is critical. The leader will energetically and enthusiastically drive his or her team to reach its goals.

If the Charismatic Style is your leadership style . . .

List times when this leadership style has worked well for you.

_____

_____

_____

_____

List times when this leadership style has not worked well for you.

_____

_____

_____

_____

Compare and contrast situations in which this style has and has not worked well. What do you notice?

_____

_____

_____

_____

(Continued on the next page)

SECTION I: LEADERSHIP STYLE SCALE

Profile Interpretation
Motivational Style

In this leadership style, the leader isn't leading. Instead, the leader puts people in a situation where they can do their best work, and then inspires them to do their best. When using this leadership style, you provide a great deal of constructive feedback, praise and motivation.

If the Motivational Style is your leadership style . . .

How do you motivate your team members?

_____

_____

_____

_____

List times when this leadership style has worked well for you.

_____

_____

_____

_____

List time when this leadership style has not worked well for you.

_____

_____

_____

_____

Leadership Role Models

Who are the leaders that you admire? (personal, famous, fictional, etc.) List them in the first column and then list why you think they are great leaders in the second column.

LEADERSHIP ROLE MODELS	WHY THEY ARE, OR MIGHT BE, ROLE MODELS

SECTION I: ACTIVITY HANDOUTS

Leadership Attributes

Regardless of the type of leadership situation you find yourself in, the necessary attributes rarely change. Think about a leadership position in which you found yourself in the past.

MY LEADERSHIP POSITION _____

(1) Creating a Vision

How did you create a vision for the final outcome for your team?

_____

_____

_____

How did you communicate your vision to the other members of the team?

_____

_____

_____

What could you have done differently?

_____

_____

_____

When you are leading your next team, how will you get people to be passionate about what they are doing so that they cannot wait to get started?

_____

_____

_____

Leadership Attributes

(2) Acting with Integrity

Acting with integrity means acting based on a personal code of conduct related to your values.

What do you value when it comes to leading others?

_____

_____

_____

How are your values represented in your vision for the team?

_____

_____

_____

What are your core values? (benevolence, fairness, morality, etc.)

_____

_____

_____

What core values do you associate with good leadership?

_____

_____

_____

What core values are not compatible with good leadership?

_____

_____

_____

SECTION I: ACTIVITY HANDOUTS

Leadership Attributes

(3) Motivating Others

Motivating others involves believing in others and inspiring them. Team leaders can motivate others by getting them to appreciate your vision for the task at hand and allowing them to feel ownership for their part as a team member. Team leaders can motivate team members by putting them in a position on the team to succeed, by communicating effectively and succinctly, and being detail-oriented in managing the tasks of the team. How did you accomplish that in each of the areas listed below?

HOW THE TEAM NEEDED MOTIVATION	HOW I MOTIVATED THOSE I WAS LEADING
To take calculated risks	
To increase choice and decision-making for team members	
To accept more responsibility	
To believe in other members of the team	
To increase interactions among team members	
To complete assigned tasks	
To activate team members	
To celebrate team members' accomplishments	
To envision the future	

SECTION I: ACTIVITY HANDOUTS

Leadership Attributes

(4) Delivering Results

In today's business world, and society in general, the *bottom line* is most important. There is less tolerance for failure and little margin for error. While they are leading, good leaders need to think about how they will produce and deliver results.

How were you and your team able to demonstrate tangible results?

_____
_____
_____
_____
_____
_____

How could you and your team have improved on these results?

_____
_____
_____
_____
_____

What type of results were the hardest to produce?

_____
_____
_____
_____
_____

The Leader in You

It is important for you to explore how much you want to continue, assume, increase, or decrease your leadership responsibilities in the various roles that you play. Answer the following questions to see how balanced you are in expressing the leader in you.

Worker/Volunteer

Do you see yourself taking on more or fewer leadership roles at work? Why and how?

_____

_____

How will this decision affect your career development?

_____

_____

Significant Other

Does your significant other appreciate and/or respect your attention to your role as a leader?

_____

_____

Will this person be supportive and understanding if you take on additional leadership responsibility?

_____

_____

How much do you want this person to be involved?

_____

_____

(Continued on the next page)

The Leader in You *(Continued)*

Caretaking

How will your increased/decreased responsibilities as a leader affect your family?

_____

_____

How do your family members view your taking on additional leadership responsibilities?

_____

_____

Personal

What personal satisfaction/rewards do you get from being a leader?

_____

_____

What types of skills do you need to develop to be a leader, or be more effective as a leader?

_____

_____

Characteristics

How do you handle yourself in unexpected or uncomfortable situations? How does this help you or hurt you in being a leader?

_____

_____

How do you like to communicate with others when you are a leader?

_____

_____

Good leaders are able to make thoughtful decisions. How would you describe your decision-making style?

_____

_____

Good leaders are enthusiastic. What types of issues are you enthusiastic about? The environment? Kids health and wellness? Education? Employment? etc.?

_____

_____

SECTION I: JOURNALING ACTIVITIES

Future Leaderships

In what ways do you see yourself becoming more of a leader?

_____
_____
_____
_____
_____

When do you see this happening?

_____
_____
_____
_____
_____

Where do you see this happening?

_____
_____
_____
_____
_____

How do you acknowledge this development to yourself?

_____
_____
_____
_____
_____

Situational Leadership

Factors to consider when leading a team:

- Skill level of the members of your team

- Experience of the members of your team

- Task — new or routine?

- Organizational environment — conservative or adventurous?

- Your unique leadership style

- Time you have to complete the task

SECTION I: EDUCATIONAL HANDOUTS

Leadership Quotes

"Leadership is the art of getting someone else to do something you want done because he or she wants to do it."

Dwight D. Eisenhower

"Leaders are the ones who keep faith with the past, keep step with the present, and keep the promise of posterity."

Jesse Jackson

"Leadership and learning are indispensable to each other."

John F. Kennedy

"A leader takes people where they want to go. A great leader takes people where they don't necessarily want to go, but ought to be."

Rosalynn Carter

"Great necessities call forth great leaders."

Abigail Adams

"Keep your fears to yourself, but share your inspiration with others."

Robert Louis Stevenson

"Leadership is not magnetic personality, that can just as well be glib tongue. It is not making friends and influencing people, that is flattery. Leadership is lifting a person's vision to higher sights, the raising of a person's performance to a higher standard, the building of a personality beyond its normal limits."

Peter F. Drucker

SECTION II:
Work Stress Scale

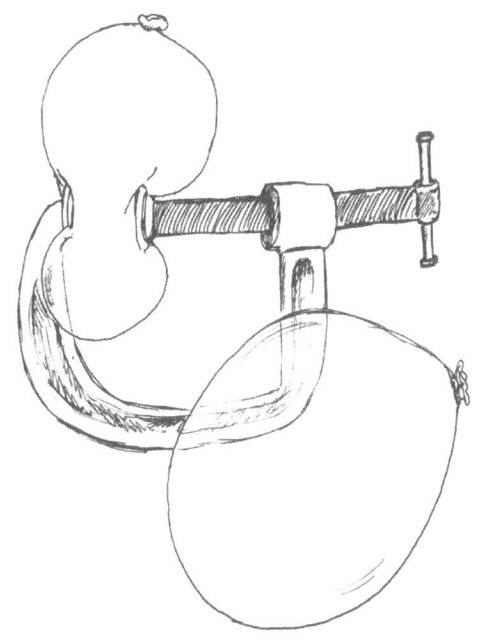

NAME _____ DATE _____

Before completing these scales, decide whether you want to respond to the scale based on your *current* work situation or one you had in the *past*. The work can be a job, a part-time job, volunteer work in your community, work at home, work with your family, a contractual situation or any other time where you are responsible for completing certain tasks. Write that work below. Refer to this work throughout these scales.

WORK _____

Work Stress Scale Directions

The characteristics of work stress increase your chances of experiencing personal stress. Work stress is the result of harmful physical and emotional responses that occur when the requirements of your task do not match your resources to do that task, your time, budget, abilities and interests, or your needs. Work stress can be a major source of anxiety, tension, and even burnout. The Work Stress Scale is designed to help you identify the sources of stress in your current or past situation.

This scale contains 32 statements divided into four categories. Read each of the statements and decide how descriptive the statement is of you at this time, or if you are not working now, at your last work situation. In each of the choices listed, circle the number of your response on the line to the right of each statement.

In the following example, the circled 1 indicates the statement is not at all descriptive of the person completing the inventory:

	A Lot Like Me	Somewhat Like Me	A Little Like Me	Not Like Me
When it comes to my work . . .				
1. I often have to work at home to finish	4	3	2	(1)

This is not a test and there are no right or wrong answers. Do not spend too much time thinking about your answers. Your initial response will likely be the most true for you.

Be sure to respond to every statement.

(Turn to the next page and begin)

SECTION II: WORK STRESS SCALE

Work Stress Scale

	A Lot Like Me	Somewhat Like Me	A Little Like Me	Not Like Me
I. When it comes to my work . . .				
I often have to work at home to finish	4	3	2	1
It often interferes with my personal life	4	3	2	1
I do not have the resources to complete all my assignments	4	3	2	1
My supervisor gives me too many assignments	4	3	2	1
I feel like my work never ends	4	3	2	1
At times, the amount of work I have is impossible for one person to do	4	3	2	1
I often work through my lunch time	4	3	2	1
The performance standards are too high in my work	4	3	2	1

Total = _____

	A Lot Like Me	Somewhat Like Me	A Little Like Me	Not Like Me
II. When it comes to my work . . .				
Others I work with are not clear about what I do	4	3	2	1
My supervisor gives me incomplete assignments	4	3	2	1
My boss often does not know what he or she wants	4	3	2	1
I am often unclear about what my boss expects from me	4	3	2	1
I am often uncertain of what my work duties are	4	3	2	1
I lack deadlines for completing assignments	4	3	2	1
I am not always sure who my supervisor is	4	3	2	1
I am unsure about the daily responsibilities of my work	4	3	2	1

Total = _____

(Continued on the next page)

SECTION II: WORK STRESS SCALE

(**Work Stress Scale** continued)

	A Lot Like Me	Somewhat Like Me	A Little Like Me	Not Like Me
III. When it comes to my work . . .				
I often have too little to do	4	3	2	1
My work situation demands that I do too many routine tasks	4	3	2	1
I feel my skills are not being used	4	3	2	1
I often do work for more than one supervisor	4	3	2	1
The work is too challenging for me	4	3	2	1
I feel overqualified for the work I do	4	3	2	1
I often feel unappreciated at work	4	3	2	1
I often feel bored at work	4	3	2	1

Total = _____

	A Lot Like Me	Somewhat Like Me	A Little Like Me	Not Like Me
IV. When it comes to my work . . .				
I often wish I had more time to spend with family and friends	4	3	2	1
I often wish I had more time to spend on my favorite hobbies	4	3	2	1
I do not have the authority to carry out certain responsibilities	4	3	2	1
I am not communicating well with my family and friends	4	3	2	1
I am unable to take care of my family because of my work	4	3	2	1
I am not able to control how I do my work	4	3	2	1
I am often given assignments I do not want	4	3	2	1
I must do things that are against my best judgment	4	3	2	1

Total = _____

(Go to the Scoring Directions on the next page)

© 2010 WHOLE PERSON ASSOCIATES, 101 WEST 2ND ST., SUITE 203, DULUTH MN 55802 ▪ 800-247-6789

SECTION II: WORK STRESS SCALE

Work Stress Scale Scoring Directions

Numerous research studies and surveys confirm that work stress is by far the leading source of anxiety for most people, and work stress will likely continue to increase over the next decade. The Work Stress Scale is designed to measure the amount of stress you are experiencing at your work, or how much you experienced at your last place of work. The scale will also help you identify the type of work stress you are experiencing. For each of the four sections, count the scores you circled for each of the items. Put that total on the line marked "Total" at the end of each section.

Then, transfer your totals to the spaces below:

ROLE OVERLOAD   TOTAL = _____

ROLE AMBIGUITY   TOTAL = _____

ROLE INCOMPATIBILITY   TOTAL = _____

ROLE CONFLICT   TOTAL = _____

Profile Interpretation

TOTAL SCALES SCORES	RESULT	INDICATIONS
Scores from 25 to 32	High	Scores from 25 to 32 on any single scale indicate that you experience a great deal of stress in that aspect of your work. Developing effective work stress management skills would be very important for you.
Scores from 16 to 24	Moderate	Scores from 16 to 24 on any single scale indicate that you experience some stress in that aspect of your work. It might be helpful to develop some additional work stress management skills to deal effectively with current changes as well as future changes.
Scores from 8 to 15	Low	Scores from 8 to 15 on any single scale indicate that you are not currently experiencing a lot of stress in your work at this time. Continue to develop effective work stress management skills in anticipation of changes that might occur.

Work Stress Scale I: Role Overload

Role Overload occurs when one has too much to do in the time available. If this happens occasionally, one can adapt. If, however, it persists over long periods of time, it can cause burnout and lead to mental, physical and work performance problems. Another common cause of role overload is when the supervisor has extremely high expectations of you. Role overload can lead to high amounts of stress. At work it can lead to low confidence, low work satisfaction, high absenteeism and high accident rates.

How can you redefine your role at work?

_____

_____

_____

_____

How does your workload compare to others' workloads in the organization?

_____

_____

_____

_____

What expectations does your supervisor have of you? In what ways are these expectations realistic? Unrealistic?

_____

_____

_____

_____

(Continued on the next page)

SECTION II: WORK STRESS SCALE

Work Stress Scale I: Role Overload *(Continued)*

What capabilities are you not using at work?

_____
_____
_____

How can you tell your supervisor that you have too much work to do?

_____
_____
_____

What can you do to manage your time better?

_____
_____
_____

How is your work interfering with your personal life?

_____
_____
_____

How can you use your energy more effectively at work?

_____
_____
_____

: WORK STRESS SCALE

Work Stress Scale II: Role Ambiguity

Role Ambiguity occurs when one lacks clarity about a particular role. It occurs when one is uncertain about what to do, when to do it and why one is doing it. Ambiguity can arise about responsibilities, the rules and regulations, the supervisor's evaluation of the performance, sources of organizational authority and work security. Role ambiguity can lead to a variety of adverse conditions including depression, anxiety and feelings of resentment. Ambiguity can occur with changes in personnel and the addition of new technology. Ambiguity can also result from poor communication between oneself and the supervisor.

What part of your role do you not understand?

_____
_____
_____
_____

What types of things do you not understand about your work?

_____
_____
_____
_____

What can your supervisor do to make your work tasks more clear?

_____
_____
_____
_____

(Continued on the next page)

SECTION II: WORK STRESS SCALE

Work Stress Scale II: Role Ambiguity *(Continued)*

How can you communicate to your supervisor that you are unclear about certain aspects of your work?

_____
_____
_____

Describe your work responsibilities in detail.

_____
_____
_____

How can you tell or demonstrate your work and/or obligations to others in your organization?

_____
_____
_____

What changes have occurred in your organization that have increased your work stress?

_____
_____
_____

Do you lack information? What types of information? How can you find the information you need to feel less stress?

_____
_____

Work Stress Scale III: Role Incompatibility

Role Incompatibility occurs when:

- there is too little variety in work tasks or too much variety
- there is too little to do or too much
- the work is too challenging or not challenging enough
- the work feels too stimulating or not stimulating enough.

If your skills and talents do not match the job description you could be:

- bored and feeling menial, like your time and capabilities are wasted
- frustrated and overwhelmed – having work you cannot complete adequately.

Either way, you probably do not feel valued by your supervisor or by the organization.

Why do you feel you are not valued by the organization?

_____
_____
_____
_____

What position within the organization would you like to be doing?

_____
_____
_____
_____

How would this task/job allow you to use your talents and skills more efficiently?

_____
_____
_____
_____

(Continued on the next page)

SECTION II: WORK STRESS SCALE

Work Stress Scale III: Role Incompatibility
(Continued)

How can you show your supervisor that you are capable of doing other work?

_____

_____

_____

Prepare a list of ways your previously untapped talents will help the organization thrive.

_____

_____

_____

Describe how your ideal work day would be spent.

_____

_____

_____

Why do you feel unappreciated at work?

_____

_____

_____

What work/tasks within the organization would you like to be doing?

_____

_____

_____

How would these tasks/work allow you to use your skills more efficiently?

_____

_____

_____

(Continued on the next page)

Work Stress Scale III: Role Incompatibility
(Continued)

Being able to use and be appreciated for one's skills is a large part of working. Unless adequately using skills, one will feel like the work is meaningless and not stimulating. In the table that follows, list in the left-hand column those skills that you are using or have been using in your work, and in the right-hand column list those skills that you have, but have not been using.

SKILLS I AM/WAS USING	SKILLS I AM/WAS NOT USING

SECTION II: WORK STRESS SCALE

Work Stress Scale IV: Role Conflict

Role Conflict occurs when one has unreasonable or incompatible expectations associated with two or more roles. Meeting the expectations associated with one role often results in failing to meet the expectations of others from the second role. People in one of the roles will get hurt or be disappointed when they have certain expectations. In today's workplace, most people feel a conflict between their work and family roles. One probably feels as if there is not enough quality time to spend with family and friends. Role conflict may also occur because one is asked to do assignments that are in conflict with his or her values and ethical principles.

How does your work interfere with your personal life?

_____
_____
_____
_____
_____

What effects of this stress do you see in the work you are doing?

_____
_____
_____
_____
_____

What can you do at work to insure that you have more quality time to spend outside of work?

_____
_____
_____
_____

(Continued on the next page)

Work Stress Scale IV: Role Conflict *(Continued)*

How does your family life impact your work role?

_____

_____

_____

Who does your work role conflict hurt the most? Why? In what ways?

_____

_____

_____

What types of things would you be doing if you did not have to work so much?

_____

_____

_____

How can you gain greater control of your work responsibilities?

_____

_____

_____

What types of things can you do at work to insure that you accomplish your work more efficiently?

_____

_____

_____

SECTION II: ACTIVITY HANDOUTS

Stress Management in the Workplace

1) Putting things into perspective

Remember that work is just one segment of your life and that family and friends are very important. You may need to find ways to energize yourself and de-escalate the stress you are experiencing. In the table that follows, in the left-hand column, list some leisure activities that you do or could engage in that could help you reduce work stress. In the right-hand column, list how these activities help you reduce stress.

LEISURE ACTIVITIES I ENJOY	HOW THE ACTIVITIES REDUCE STRESS

2) Modify Your Work Situation

What are some of the ways that you could tailor your work better to your skills?
Are there opportunities for lateral transfers?

_____

_____

(Continued on the next page)

Stress Management in the Workplace *(Continued)*

3) Take Time Away From Your Work

When you feel that the stress is building, it helps to find ways to take a break. Walking away from the situation, going outside and taking a short walk is one way to get away from the stress. What are some of the things you can do when you begin to feel stressed at work?

_____

_____

_____

4) Don't Over-Commit Yourself

Be careful to avoid scheduling things back-to-back or trying to do too much in one day. Try to distinguish those things you "must" do at your work and those that you "should" do. Elevate the "must" things to the top of your priority list.

Musts at Work	**"Shoulds" at Work**
_____	_____
_____	_____
_____	_____
_____	_____
_____	_____

5) Delegate Responsibility

If you are feeling overworked, are there things you could delegate to others to do? What might those be?

_____

_____

_____

SECTION II: JOURNALING ACTIVITIES

Work Stress 101

What types of work stress are you experiencing most and why?

_____
_____
_____
_____
_____
_____
_____

What people in your life are most affected by your stress?

_____
_____
_____
_____
_____
_____
_____

How are they affected?

_____
_____
_____
_____
_____
_____
_____

SECTION II: JOURNALING ACTIVITIES

Stress Management

How will you begin to manage your work stress better?

_____
_____
_____
_____
_____
_____
_____
_____
_____
_____

What aspects of the other stress-management techniques will you try?

_____
_____
_____
_____
_____
_____
_____
_____
_____

Warning Signs of Work Stress

- Absenteeism

- Anger Management Issues

- Anxiety

- Burnout

- Concentration Difficulties

- Depression

- Fatigue

- Work dissatisfaction

- Low Morale

- Physical Problems (headaches, stomach problems)

- Sleep Disturbances

Work Stress Statistics*

- 80% of all workers feel stress and nearly half say they need help in learning to manage it.

- 40% of all workers feel their work is very or extremely stressful.

- 26% of all workers say they are burned out by their work.

- Work stress is more strongly associated with health complaints than financial or family problems.

- 14% of all workers say they felt like striking a co-worker during the past year.

- 25% of all workers say they felt like screaming or shouting because of work stress during the past year.

- 10% say they were concerned that a co-worker might become violent.

*Adapted from report from the National Institute for Occupational Safety and Health titled *Stress management in work settings.* http://www.cdc.gov/niosh/pdfs/87-111.pdf

SECTION III:
Cultural Competency Scale

NAME _____   DATE _____

Before completing these scales, decide whether you want to respond to the scale based on your *current* work situation or one you had in the *past*. The work can be a job, a part-time job, volunteer work in your community, work at home, work with your family, a contractual situation or any other time where you are responsible for completing certain tasks. Write that work below. Refer to this work throughout these scales.

WORK _____

SECTION III: CULTURAL COMPETENCY SCALE

Cultural Competency Scale Directions

Cultural competency is defined as a set of attitudes, interests and skills that enable you to effectively work, play and study with people who are culturally different from you. The Cultural Competency Scale is designed to assess your competencies in working with people from different cultures, allow you to explore your thoughts and feelings about people different from you and teach you some skills for more effectively working with people from cultures different from yours.

Read each of the statements that follow and decide how much the statement describes you. Then, circle the number of your response on the line to the right of each statement. In the following example, the circled 2 indicates that the statement is Somewhat True for the person completing the scale:

	3 = Very True	2 = Somewhat True	1 = Not True
I. ATTITUDES			
I consider ways in which people from different cultures view things in different ways (e.g., alone time, family, etc.)	3	(2)	1

This is not a test and there are no right or wrong answers. Do not spend too much time thinking about your answers. Your initial response will likely be the most true for you.

Be sure to respond to every statement.

(Turn to the next page and begin)

SECTION III: CULTURAL COMPETENCY SCALE

Cultural Competency Scale

	3 = Very True	2 = Somewhat True	1 = Not True
I. ATTITUDES			
I consider ways in which people from different cultures view things in different ways (e.g., alone time, family, etc.).	3	2	1
I make an effort to get to know people from a variety of cultures.	3	2	1
I accept and respect differences in people who are different from me.	3	2	1
I am aware of how cultural differences influence thoughts, behaviors, and communication.	3	2	1
I accept how the global marketplace has changed society.	3	2	1
I do not stereotype people based solely on the culture from which they come.	3	2	1

ATTITUDES TOTAL = _____

II. KNOWLEDGE

I am interested in knowing how my culture is viewed by others.	3	2	1
I am interested in reading about other cultures.	3	2	1
I am interested in learning about cultures different from my own.	3	2	1
I am interested in visiting other countries.	3	2	1
I like to share my knowledge and experiences with people from other cultures.	3	2	1
I would like to learn more about a variety of cultural norms, attitudes and beliefs.	3	2	1

KNOWLEDGE TOTAL = _____

(Continued on the next page)

SECTION III: CULTURAL COMPETENCY SCALE

(**Cultural Competency Scale** continued)

	3 = Very True	2 = Somewhat True	1 = Not True
III. SKILLS			
I am able to communicate with people from cultures different from mine	3	2	1
I am aware of how my actions affect people from other cultures	3	2	1
I enjoy making friends with people of different cultures	3	2	1
I am willing to adapt my behaviors to fit a variety of cultural norms	3	2	1
I am aware of, and can use, a variety of nonverbal communication patterns in my interactions with people from cultures different from mine	3	2	1
I am flexible and respect others' views, even if they are different from my own	3	2	1

SKILLS TOTAL = _____

	3 = Very True	2 = Somewhat True	1 = Not True
IV. VALUING DIVERSITY			
I like to establish working relationships with people from different cultures	3	2	1
I am interested in learning phrases in another language so I can interact better	3	2	1
I would attend a workshop to learn about the beliefs of a different culture	3	2	1
I feel very comfortable in cross-cultural situations	3	2	1
I enjoy working with people who are from a different culture	3	2	1
I would/do enjoy attending different cultural events or festivals	3	2	1

VALUING DIVERSITY TOTAL = _____

(Go to the Scoring Directions on the next page)

SECTION III: CULTURAL COMPETENCY SCALE

Cultural Competency Scale
Scoring Directions

Cultural competence refers to the ability to work effectively with people from different ethnic and cultural backgrounds. To determine your cultural competence, add the numbers you have circled for each of the four sections you just completed. You will get a number from 6 to 18. Put that total on the line marked total at the end of each section. Then, transfer your totals to the spaces below:

ATTITUDES: _____

KNOWLEDGE: _____

SKILLS: _____

VALUING DIVERSITY: _____

Profile Interpretation

TOTAL SCALES SCORES	RESULT	INDICATIONS
Scores from 15 to 18	High	Scores from 15 to 18 on any single scale indicates that you currently possess many attitudes, knowledge, skills and values needed to recognize and appreciate diversity. Continue to further develop effective cultural competencies to work effectively in the global economy.
Scores from 10 to 14	Moderate	Scores from 10 to 14 on any single scale indicates that you currently possess some attitudes, knowledge, skills and values needed to recognize and appreciate diversity. Continue to develop even more effective cultural competencies to work effectively in the global economy.
Scores from 6 to 9	Low	Scores from 6 to 9 on any single scale indicates that you do not currently possess the attitudes, knowledge, skills and values needed to recognize and appreciate diversity. You need to continue to develop effective cultural competencies to work effectively in the global economy.

SECTION III: CULTURAL COMPETENCY SCALE

Cultural Competency Scale Profile Descriptions

Following are descriptions of the four scales included on the Cultural Competency Scale. Remember that as globalization becomes the norm, people skilled in building effective relationships with diverse co-workers, supervisors and customers will be the most sought after.

Attitudes – People scoring low on this scale may not have learned the importance of curiosity, empathy and respect in cross-cultural communications. They may still have some stereotypes of particular cultures based on past experiences and do not make much of an effort to learn about other cultures.

Knowledge – People scoring low on this scale tend not to be interested in learning about the customs and traditions of other cultures, are not interested in visiting other cultures to learn about them and are not interested in sharing experiences to learn about people from other cultures.

Skills – People scoring low on this scale may have trouble communicating and making friends with people from other cultures. They are rigid about their beliefs of people from other cultures and may have difficulty valuing the views and opinions of people different from them.

Valuing diversity – People scoring low on this scale may have difficulty accepting and respecting differences in people. They have a hard time accepting that people come from very different backgrounds, and that their values, traditions, ways of communicating, thoughts, customs and institutions differ.

The following sections contain exercises to help you more effectively build relationships with diverse people in the workplace. Regardless of your scores on the scale, these exercises will help you to become a better employee and citizen in the global economy.

SECTION III: ACTIVITY HANDOUTS

Valuing Diversity

Being able to recognize that diversity exists and being able to value the fundamental differences that exist between cultures is almost a necessary requirement for working successfully in today's global economy. Most workplaces today believe that the goal is for all employees to work together to achieve mutual goals and to accomplish this is to recognize that cultural diversity exists. Everyone needs to learn to value and respect the differences that people bring to the workplace. In the table below, list some of the fundamental benefits of having diverse co-workers in the left-hand column and list the obstacles of having diverse co-workers in the right-hand column.

BENEFITS OF HAVING DIVERSE CO-WORKERS	OBSTACLES TO GETTING ALONG WITH DIVERSE CO-WORKERS

Interact with Diverse Individuals

In order to enhance your cultural competency, continue (or begin) to interact with people who are different from you. When people are brought together to complete a task, their supervisors hope they will begin to form a relationship that will dissolve stereotypes and enhance cooperative interaction. In the table below, list some the people (work, school, community, etc.) whom you would like to get to know better. In the column on the left, list these people and in the column on the right, list an activity, project, or mutual goal that you and the other person could work toward. Then, "just do it!"

PERSON I WOULD LIKE TO GET TO KNOW	PROJECT, ACTIVITY, TASK WE COULD WORK ON

SECTION III: ACTIVITY HANDOUTS

Understand Your Own Cultural Identity

To appreciate the unique heritage of others, you may need to develop an appreciation of your own unique cultural and ethnic identity. In the spaces below, identify some of the characteristics that make you unique.

PERSONAL CHARACTERISTICS	HOW IT MAKES ME UNIQUE
Where I was born	
My religious upbringing	
My gender	
My occupation/past occupations	
My age	
My socio-economic status	
My partner (present and past)	

Avoid Stereotyping

A stereotype is a fixed impression of someone, or exaggerated or preconceived ideas about particular social groups. Some of the general elements of stereotypical behavior are that they serve as a foundation for discrimination, they are detrimental to productivity in the workplace, they create an obstacle to getting to know others, they remain until they are tested and challenged, and they are based on differences in such factors as appearance, religion, socio-economic status, occupation, ethnicity, race, gender and disability.

Stereotypes usually surface in these ways:

- Simplified negative or positive ideas about a person

- Overgeneralizations that do not represent all members of a group

- Attempts to enhance one's own self-esteem

Suggestions to minimizing and changing your stereotypes:

- Interact with co-workers on a personal as well as professional level. The more you are able to interact with people dissimilar from you, the less you will stereotype.

- Make a commitment of time to developing relationships with people different from you. Maintain an open mind.

- Volunteer for projects that will include diverse co-workers.

- Work to form an accurate impression of other people.

SECTION III: ACTIVITY HANDOUTS

My Stereotypes

Now is the time to clarify what different types of stereotypes you hold. In the table that follows, think about the stereotypes that you hold, whether positive or negative, about some of the people with whom you typically interact. In the left-hand column are some of the groups that have stereotypes associated with them. In the right-hand column, identify and list some of your stereotypes you associate with the group of people.

Your comments on this particular page are yours alone and do not need to be shared.

GROUPS	MY STEREOTYPES
Males	
Females	
Gender orientation	
African Americans	
Asian Americans	
European Americans	
Hispanic Americans	
Native Americans	

(Continued on the next page)

(My Stereotypes continued)

GROUPS	MY STEREOTYPES
Other Nationalities	
Anyone who does not speak or understand English well	
People with Disabilities	
Children	
Teenagers	
Older People	
People of low socio-economic status	
People from other countries	
People of religions other than my own	
Other	

SECTION III: ACTIVITY HANDOUTS

Respecting Differences

It is important to learn to collaborate with people from various cultures. For collaboration to occur, it will be helpful to become aware of cultural differences among people and places and be open-minded. Think about how you might learn more about other cultures. In the table that follows, list some of the strategies you might use to learn more about other cultures.

WAYS TO LEARN ABOUT OTHER CULTURES	STRATEGIES
Visit or learn about other countries	
Attend workshops or seminars	
Learn a foreign language	
Read about other cultures	
Talk to people from another culture	
Attend cultural festivals or activities	
Other	

SECTION III: ACTIVITY HANDOUTS

Multicultural Collaboration

As you begin to work on multicultural collaboration in your work, keep in mind:

Practice, practice, practice. That's the first rule, because it's in the doing that we actually get better at cross-cultural communication.

With whom will you be able to practice developing multicultural collaborative relationships?

_____

_____

_____

_____

Don't assume that your way is the right way to communicate. Keep questioning your assumptions about the "right way" to communicate. Research cross-cultural communication on the Internet. How do different cultures communicate in ways different from you?

_____

_____

_____

_____

Watch your body language. Postures that indicate receptivity in one culture might indicate aggressiveness in another. Notice non-verbal communication differences in cultures. How do various cultures communicate differently through body language?

_____

_____

_____

_____

(Continued on the next page)

SECTION III: ACTIVITY HANDOUTS

(Multicultural Collaboration *continued*)

Listen actively and empathetically. Try to put yourself in the other person's shoes. Especially when another person's perceptions or ideas are very different from your own, you might need to operate at the edge of your own comfort zone. How can you begin listening more actively?

_____

_____

_____

_____

_____

_____

_____

_____

Be prepared for a discussion of the past. Use this as an opportunity to develop an understanding from "the other's" point of view, rather than getting defensive or impatient. Acknowledge historical events that have taken place. Be open to learning more about them. Honest acknowledgment of the mistreatment and oppression that have taken place on the basis of cultural difference is vital for effective communication.

What types of questions could you ask about historical events that have taken place in the person's life?

_____

_____

_____

_____

_____

_____

_____

Cross-Cultural Communication

It would be impossible to talk about all of the ways to communicate effectively with people from other cultures. In this section are some tips for enhancing your cross-cultural communication.

To Communicate Effectively with People from Other Cultures

- Be aware of the possibility of cultural differences. Never assume that other people are like you.

- Be open and flexible in your communication with others.

- Acknowledge and respect the cultural differences of the people with whom you work.

- Strive to understand other people and their cultural differences. Ask questions.

Ideas for Better Cross-Cultural Communication

- Speak clearly, normal pace, normal volume and do not use colloquialisms, (i.e. 'hold the guacamole') or double negatives (i.e. 'not bad').

- Use short sentences that are clear and concise.

- Provide instructions in a clear sequence. Never assume that the other person knows what you are talking about or has done the task before.

- Summarize ideas and instructions often.

- Check for understanding - ask questions which require more than a 'yes' or 'no' answer (using who, what, where, why and how).

- Demonstrate activities or tasks if possible.

- Write instructions on a note-pad or poster if necessary.

- Make procedures very clear.

- Be aware of non-verbal signals.

- Be patient. Non-English speakers may have to translate what you've said into their first language and then try to convert their response back into English.

- Do not patronize non-English speakers. Although they might not be as adept at your language, they might be just as capable as you in the workplace.

What I Learned About Myself

What have you learned about yourself and how you interact with people different from you?

_____
_____
_____
_____
_____
_____
_____
_____
_____
_____

What have you learned about people from other cultures and how they interact with you?

_____
_____
_____
_____
_____
_____
_____
_____
_____

Cultural Competencies

Which attitudes and what knowledge do you possess to enhance your inter-cultural competencies?

_____

_____

_____

_____

_____

_____

_____

Which attitudes and knowledge do you need to work on?

_____

_____

_____

_____

_____

What skills and values do you bring to interactions with people from other cultures?

_____

_____

_____

_____

_____

SECTION III: JOURNALING ACTIVITIES

My Cultural Experiences

Whom or what people do you know from a culture different that your own?

_____
_____
_____
_____
_____
_____
_____
_____
_____
_____

What have your experiences been with those individuals?

_____
_____
_____
_____
_____
_____
_____
_____
_____
_____

SECTION III: EDUCATIONAL HANDOUTS

How Cultures Differ*

Cultures are differentiated by these parameters:

- Individualism (value is placed on individuals and their decisions) vs. Collectivism (value is placed on a group and membership in the group

- Views of time and space

- Roles of men and women

- Concepts of class and status

- Values

- Language

- Body language

- Rituals (ways of commemorating meaningful life cycle events like weddings, births, deaths and religious worship)

- Significance of work

- Beliefs about the meaning of disabilities and health issues

*Adapted from Tomoeda, C.K., & Bayles, K.A. (2002). *Cultivating cultural competence in the workplace, classroom, and clinic.* http://www.asha.org/about/publications/leader-online/archives/2002/q2/020202d.htm.

SECTION IV:
Organizational Style Scale

NAME _____   DATE _____

Before completing these scales, decide whether you want to respond to the scale based on your *current* work situation or one you had in the *past*. The work can be a job, a part-time job, volunteer work in your community, work at home, work with your family, a contractual situation or any other time where you are responsible for completing certain tasks. Write that work below. Refer to this work throughout these scales.

WORK _____

SECTION IV: ORGANIZATIONAL STYLE SCALE

Organizational Style Scale Directions

The Organizational Style Scale contains 60 words that describe various personality traits you may or may not have. To complete the scale:

Read each of the words listed and decide whether or not the word describes you. If the statement does describe you, circle the word in the column. If the statement does not describe you, do not circle the word, simply move to the next word. Circle all of the words that describe you.

In the following example, the circled words indicate that the person completing the inventory feels he or she is imaginative, technical and supportive.

I consider myself to be (circle words) . . .

(Imaginative)	Decisive	Emotional	Methodical
Idea-Oriented	(Technical)	(Supportive)	Cautious
Enthusiastic	Assertive	Trusting	Responsible

This is not a test and there are no right or wrong answers. Do not spend too much time thinking about your answers. Your initial response will likely be the most true for you.

Be sure to respond to every statement.

(Turn to the next page and begin)

SECTION IV: ORGANIZATIONAL STYLE SCALE

Organizational Style Scale

I consider myself to be (circle words) . . .

Imaginative	Decisive	Emotional	Methodical
Idea-oriented	Technical	Supportive	Cautious
Enthusiastic	Assertive	Trusting	Responsible
Risk-taker	Investigative	Warm	Focused
Visionary	Mathematical	Calm	Consistent
Adaptable	Tenacious	Cooperative	Accurate
Creative	Logical	Sympathetic	Serious
Flexible	Problem-Solver	Considerate	Punctual
Innovative	Analytical	Sensitive	Predictable
Original Thinker	Competitive	Compassionate	Organized
Adventurous	Thorough	Attentive listener	Sensible
Energetic	Systematic	Nurturing	Disciplined
Intuitive	Factual	Tolerant	Detail-Oriented
Curious	Rational	Caring	Reliable
Spontaneous	Ambitious	Attentive	Loyal
_____	_____	_____	_____
TOTAL I.	TOTAL R.	TOTAL S.	TOTAL ST.

(Go to the Scoring Directions on the next page)

SECTION IV: ORGANIZATIONAL STYLE SCALE

Organizational Style Scoring Directions

The Organizational Style Scale is designed to measure your personality type and your organizational style in the workplace. For all of the items on the previous pages, count the total number of items you circled for each column. Put that total on the line marked "Total" at the bottom of each of the four columns. Then transfer your totals to the space below:

_____ = I — Imaginative

_____ = R — Rational

_____ = S — Sensitive

_____ = ST — Structured

Profile Interpretation

The area in which you scored the highest tends to be your organizational style. Similarly, the area in which you scored the lowest tends to be your least preferred style for organizing your time and resources. Go to the section which describes your preferred organizational style. If time permits, read about the other organizational styles. If you had similar scores for several of the styles, read each of them and decide which organizational style fits you most, or how you combine the two styles in managing your time and resources in your work.

SECTION IV: ORGANIZATIONAL STYLE SCALE

Imaginative Personality Style

Personality Type

Imaginative personality types are usually innovative, inquisitive and adventurous. They are intellectually curious, appreciative of art and sensitive to beauty. They are very aware of their feelings and tend to think and act in unconventional, nonconforming ways. They have a facility for thinking in symbols and abstractions, and are extremely creative. They are idea-oriented and innovative in identifying solutions to problems. They easily become involved in creative endeavors and seem to find outlets for their imagination in a variety of roles. They value freedom and hate to feel controlled or obligated. They are spontaneous and trust their own impulses to help them make decisions. They live for a variety of experiences and feel competent in handling situations that arise and recover easily from setbacks. They like to see the tangible results of their work and will take any risks necessary to meet the challenges in their lives. They respond well to challenges and crises, but take immediate action and then quickly lose interest. They do not like rules, routines or structured work environments. They like working with practical, action oriented people.

Organizational Style

People with an Imaginative Organizational Style usually approach organization like they do everything else – in the most adventurous, artistic and non-conforming manner possible. They see the world and their work in terms of patterns that they can easily put into order. These people are excellent problem-solvers and innovative thinkers, seeing the big picture and not getting bogged down in the details. They lack organization and may sometimes lose things. They prefer originality and variety in their organizational system, and probably get bored if this system gets too inflexible.

Typical Characteristics of People with an Imaginative Organizational Style

   Entrepreneurial

   Easily sidetracked

   Enthusiastic and energetic

   Drained when dealing with details

   Visionary thinkers

   Able to visualize and daydream

   Innovative and inspirational

(Continued on the next page)

SECTION IV: ORGANIZATIONAL STYLE SCALE

Imaginative Personality Style *(Continued)*

What can you do to become less stressed?
_____
_____

How does your organizational style help you at work?
_____
_____

How does your organizational style hinder you at work?
_____
_____

How can you stop getting bogged down in task details?
_____
_____

How can you use your entrepreneurial personality to your advantage?
_____
_____
_____

How can you use a calendar, appointment book, etc., to help you be more organized?
_____
_____
_____

Rational Organizational Style

Personality Type

Rational personality types are usually very logical in all they do. They are low-keyed and prefer to work with data than with people. They are not very assertive and tend to worry about things they cannot control. When dealing with people, they tend to rely on logic rather than emotions. They are reserved and would rather work by themselves than as part of a group. They tend to strive for perfection. They are willing to spend a great deal of energy to complete projects they have started. They often get bogged down in details and "cannot see the forest for the trees." They are conscientious and are willing to work long hours to make sure things are done the way they are supposed to be done. They are often viewed by others as deep thinkers. They are quiet and forceful and take themselves very seriously. They approach life in a low-keyed, determined manner, and they are very effective in dealing with others because they make decisions only after having all the facts. They have little tolerance for carelessness in themselves and/or in others, and can be critical and impatient with others. They will analyze a situation, then proceed in the most logical manner. They are often accused of "planning" everything, and they are serious people who set many long-term goals. They enjoy making lists, using charts and figures, and focusing on every detail. They need order to function effectively. They tend to be quiet, thoughtful and analytical.

Organizational Style

Rational personality types usually believe that disorganization can cost time and money. They diligently work around the clock to ensure that tasks get done. They are interested in figuring out how things work, analyzing them and then making them functional. They have the ability for in-depth mental analysis that makes them rational, objective and efficient. They are probably admired for their focus and ability to get things done. These people are able to use diagnostic thinking and approach work from an objective perspective. They would enjoy a functional workspace in which everything is ready to go at a moment's notice.

Typical Characteristics of People with a Rational Organizational Style:

- Oriented to facts and figures
- Believe that precision is critical
- Often called "control freaks"
- Compulsive about making improvements
- Able to set and achieve goals
- Punctual and practical
- Lack effective communication skills

(Continued on the next page)

Rational Organizational Style *(Continued)*

How can you make sure you keep sight of the 'big picture' while focusing also on the details?

_____

_____

How does your organizational style help you at work?

_____

_____

How does your organizational style hinder you at work?

_____

_____

How can you stop your need to have control in the workplace?

_____

_____

What types of things do you do that you can delegate to others?

_____

_____

How can you enhance your communication skills to get more done?

_____

_____

SECTION IV: ORGANIZATIONAL STYLE SCALE

Sensitive Organizational Style

Personality Type

Sensitive personality types are warm and compassionate and have a vision for what the ideal world looks like and then they work to create that world here on earth. They are optimistic and enjoy work that allows them to use their creativity, individuality, insight and helpful nature to benefit other people. They are interested in helping other people to realize their unique potential. They are sensitive to the needs of others and are skilled at bringing out the best in others. They like to be mentally stimulated and often come with new and interesting ideas and solutions to problems. They enjoy working in friendly, conflict-free environments where personal growth and development are encouraged by supervisors. They put a great deal of energy into projects and are easily disappointed when projects or people do not turn out as expected. They genuinely want to learn about and better understand themselves and others.

Organizational Style

Sensitive personality types usually take a back seat to the relationships with people where they work. They feel alive and happiest when there are people around them. They want and enjoy a work environment that nurtures who they truly are. They manage their environment to guarantee a sense of unity and harmony with others. They seek to build goodwill with everything and everyone. They may find it difficult getting assignments completed on time or arriving at meetings in a timely way because they often forget about time. They love having fun and connecting to others and that is what is important for them in the workplace.

Typical Characteristics of People with a Sensitive Organizational Style:

Ineffective time managers

Great at nurturing relationships

Lack focus and structure

People-oriented

Sensitive

Willing to drop everything to help others

Driven by moods, not calendars

(Continued on the next page)

Sensitive Organizational Style *(Continued)*

What can you do to become more organized?

_____
_____

How does your organizational style help you at work?

_____
_____

How does your organizational style hinder you at work?

_____
_____

How can you begin to gain more focus in the workplace?

_____
_____

How do your relationships in the workplace prevent you from getting your work done?

_____
_____

How can you use a calendar, appointment book, etc. to help you be more organized?

_____
_____

SECTION IV: ORGANIZATIONAL STYLE SCALE

Structured Organizational Style

Personality Type

Structured personality types are usually realistic, practical and responsible in the way they do things. They like to be fully in charge of their specific responsibilities. They want to be valuable parts of any organization and will take on additional assignments to make a contribution. They feel like they must be the responsible one if the work is to get done. They have a strong work ethic and believe that hard work is the most important factor in being successful. They believe that they can achieve anything by simply working hard to achieve it. They serve and bring tremendous stability to any organization. They want their supervisors to judge their performance based on a specific set of work responsibilities. They do not like change, especially if they do not understand the reason for the change. They are reliable and hard-working and value common sense rather than theories, vague information or abstract thinking.

Organizational Style

Structured personality types have the ability to understand work and organization by following rules and proven routines. They have a linear, structured approach that focuses on details to help them effectively manage tasks and assignments. They do not care as much about speed as methodical precision. They have a deliberate, slow-paced style that is conservative, but effective. They like to follow the rules and routines that have worked for them in the past. They get things done at a slow, steady pace. They like having parameters including the time limits for tasks and assignments they are given.

Typical Characteristics of People with a Structured Organizational Style

Easily annoyed by interruptions

Always on time

Prone to make decisions based on previous successes

Quality oriented

Slow and careful to make decisions

In need of time to become structured

Resistant to change

(Continued on the next page)

Structured Organizational Style *(Continued)*

How does your organizational style help you at work?

_____

_____

How does your organizational style hinder you at work?

_____

_____

What can you do to be less stressed by interruptions?

_____

_____

How does your need for quality restrict you from achieving more?

_____

_____

How can you be more flexible in the workplace?

_____

_____

Why do you think you are resistant to change?

_____

_____

SECTION IV: ACTIVITY HANDOUTS

Daily To-Do Lists

To-do lists can help you identify tasks and assignments that need to be completed, motivate you to remember them and work toward accomplishing them. Making "to-do" lists eventually become a habit that can help you remain organized in the workplace. To begin with, think about important things you need to do tomorrow and complete the planning worksheet provided below. List the tasks you need to complete, phone calls you need to make to people and appointments you need to keep. As you complete the tasks, place a check mark in the "Completed" column.

DAILY TO-DO LIST

Time	Tasks to Complete	Phone Calls to Make	Appointments to Keep	Completed
7:00 am				
8:00 am				
9:00 am				
10:00 am				
11:00 am				
12 Noon				
1:00 pm				
2:00 pm				
3:00 pm				
4:00 pm				
5:00 pm				
6:00 pm				
7:00 pm				

Prioritizing a Weekly To-Do List

In the table below, think about your next work week and write down everything that needs to be done. After listing tasks, prioritize by numbering them according to their importance in the box on the right of each item. Prioritizing is identifying the various tasks that are most important and giving those tasks more of your time, energy and attention.

Things I need to do this week	Number

SECTION IV: ACTIVITY HANDOUTS

Priority List

List your tasks for next week based on their priority. This process can be used in the workplace to help you become more organized and efficient.

High Priority Tasks
Low Priority Tasks

SECTION IV: ACTIVITY HANDOUTS

Next Week's List

Now you are ready to make a list for next week. Check with your priority list to be sure you've put high priorities first. Then place a check mark once you have it completed. Write YES or NO based on whether follow-up is needed.

Day	Task	Completed	Follow-up Needed?
Monday			
Tuesday			
Wednesday			
Thursday			
Friday			
Saturday			
Sunday			

© 2010 WHOLE PERSON ASSOCIATES, 101 WEST 2ND ST., SUITE 203, DULUTH MN 55802 ▪ 800-247-6789

SECTION IV: JOURNALING ACTIVITIES

Organizational Styles

My Style: _____

How can you use your organizational style(s) to your benefit?

_____

_____

_____

_____

_____

_____

_____

_____

_____

What do you wish you could change about your present organizational style(s)? How can you begin this change?

_____

_____

_____

_____

_____

_____

_____

_____

I Wish

What personality or organizational trait (from the other three organizational styles) do you wish you had?

_____
_____
_____
_____
_____
_____
_____
_____
_____

What aspects of your organizational style do you wish you did not have?

_____
_____
_____
_____
_____
_____
_____
_____
_____

Organizing Tools

CALENDAR

- desk organizer
- wall organizer
- hand-held organizer or computer

DAY PLANNER (small enough to carry with you)

- generic appointment book
- "to-do" list
- goal-setter

ELECTRONIC DEVICES

Interesting Organizational Statistics*

- People spend the equivalent of four days every year looking for things.

- Eighty percent of what you file you never look at again.

- Two million tons of junk mail are delivered every day.

- Eight percent of documents are eventually lost.

- Lost pieces of paper are moved nine times before they are acted upon.

- Every day the Internet carries over 281 billion e-mails and growing.

- The use of office paper has tripled since the birth of the computer

*Adapted from Nakone, L. (2005). *Organizing for your brain type.* New York, NY: St. Martin's Press.

SECTION V:
Work-Leisure Balance Scale

NAME _____ DATE _____

Before completing these scales, decide whether you want to respond to the scale based on your *current* work situation or one you had in the *past*. The work can be a job, a part-time job, volunteer work in your community, work at home, work with your family, a contractual situation or any other time where you are responsible for completing certain tasks. Write that work below. Refer to this work throughout these scales.

WORK _____

SECTION V: WORK-LEISURE BALANCE SCALE

Work-Leisure Balance Scale Directions

Your career is a combination of the work you do and the various types of leisure activities in which you engage. People view and define work and leisure differently. Work is a major source of life satisfaction for some people; for others, work is an obligation. Some people spend most of their time engaging in leisure activities while work is all-consuming for others. The Work-Leisure Balance Scale measures your commitment to work and leisure.

This scale contains thirty-five statements. Read each statement and decide how the response best describes you. In each of the choices, circle the number of your response on the right of the statement.

In the following example, the circled 3 indicates the statement is somewhat like the person completing the scale.

4 = A lot like me   3 = Somewhat like me   2 = A little like me   1 = Not like me

Example:

1. I like my work better than my leisure activities 4   (3)   2   1

This is not a test and there are no right or wrong answers. Do not spend too much time thinking about your answers. Your initial response will likely be the most true for you. Be sure to respond to every statement.

(Turn to the next page and begin)

SECTION V: WORK-LEISURE BALANCE SCALE

Work-Leisure Balance scale

4 = A lot like me   3 = Somewhat like me   2 = A little like me   1 = Not like me

Career Commitment

1. I like my work better than my leisure activities	4	3	2	1
2. My life revolves around my work	4	3	2	1
3. I live, eat and breathe my work	4	3	2	1
4. Work is more important than most other things in my life	4	3	2	1
5. The majority of my satisfaction comes from work-related activities	4	3	2	1
6. I am driven to succeed at my work	4	3	2	1
7. I feel pressure to be productive at work	4	3	2	1

Career Commitment = _____

Work Involvement

8. I work more hours than most people	4	3	2	1
9. I would rather work than take time off for a vacation	4	3	2	1
10. I take work home with me on the weekends and at night	4	3	2	1
11. I am often too tired to eat when I get home from work	4	3	2	1
12. I spend a great deal of time at my work	4	3	2	1
13. I often do not take a lunch break from work	4	3	2	1
14. Most of my friends are business colleagues/co-workers	4	3	2	1

Work Involvement = _____

(Continued on the next page)

SECTION V: WORK-LEISURE BALANCE SCALE

(**Work-Leisure Balance Scale** *continued*)

4 = A lot like me   3 = Somewhat like me   2 = A little like me   1 = Not like me

Personality Type

	4	3	2	1
15. I push myself to meet deadlines	4	3	2	1
16. I am intense about my work	4	3	2	1
17. I am more assertive than most people	4	3	2	1
18. I am results oriented	4	3	2	1
19. I tend to get bored more easily than most people	4	3	2	1
20. I thrive on activities that require my full attention and concentration	4	3	2	1
21. I work and play hard	4	3	2	1

Personality Type = _____

Time Manager

22. I am driven by a feeling of lack of time	4	3	2	1
23. I feel that I cannot accomplish what I want in the time I have	4	3	2	1
24. I feel guilty when I take time off to have fun	4	3	2	1
25. I am very impatient	4	3	2	1
26. I feel frustrated when I am not in total control	4	3	2	1
27. I set long-range goals and work to achieve them	4	3	2	1
28. I plan my time well	4	3	2	1

Time Manager = _____

(Continued on the next page)

SECTION V: WORK-LEISURE BALANCE SCALE

(**Work-Leisure Balance Scale** continued)

4 = A lot like me   3 = Somewhat like me   2 = A little like me   1 = Not like me

Leisure Style

29. I have trouble finding fulfilling leisure activities	4	3	2	1
30. I feel guilty when I'm relaxing	4	3	2	1
31. My leisure activities are related to my work.	4	3	2	1
32. I read work-related magazines and books in my leisure time	4	3	2	1
33. When I do engage in leisure activities, I am competitive and expect to win or be the best	4	3	2	1
34. I require less leisure time than most people	4	3	2	1
35. I exercise for health reasons rather than enjoyment	4	3	2	1

Leisure Style = _____

(Go to the Scoring Directions on the next page)

SECTION V: WORK-LEISURE BALANCE SCALE

Work-Leisure Balance Scale
Scoring Directions

The scale you have just completed will help you identify the importance of work in your life and how successfully you are, or have been, at balancing your work and leisure. For each of the sections on the previous pages, count the scores you circled for each of the five sections. Put that total on the line marked "Total" at the end of each section.

Use the spaces below to transfer your scores to each of the scales below. Then total the scores and put that number on the GRAND TOTAL line.

TOTALS

Career Commitment measures your commitment to your career   _____

Work Involvement measures your involvement in the work you do   _____

Personality Type measures your personality characteristics
as they relate to work   _____

Time Manager measures your desire to be successful in the
shortest amount of time possible   _____

Leisure Style measures your interest in leisure as a source
of relaxation and life satisfaction   _____

GRAND TOTAL = _____

After you have completed the transferring of your total scores, see the Profile Interpretation in the section that follows for more information.

SECTION V: WORK-LEISURE BALANCE SCALE

Profile Interpretation

In the table that follows, find the range of your scores on each of the scales and use the information to assist you in the interpretation of your scores.

TOTAL SCALES SCORES	RESULT	INDICATIONS
Scores from 22 to 28	High	Scores from 22 to 28 on any scale indicates that you are driven to achieve success in your work. You spend most of your time in work-related activities. You may even feel guilty or depressed when you are unable to work. You devote high levels of energy and time to your work. Unless you burnout from working too much, you will be able to accomplish many goals and assignments.
Scores from 14 to 21	Moderate	Scores from 14 to 21 on any scale indicates that you are able to balance work with other roles such as leisure and family/friends. You place as much importance in work as most people who have taken the scale. You are able to use leisure as a way of making your work less stressful and life more enjoyable.
Scores from 7 to 13	Low	Scores from 7 to 13 on any single scale indicates that you tend to be less driven to achieve at your work. You are primarily interested in pursuing activities involving leisure and family. You may be a good worker, but work is simply a way for you to make a living so that you can pursue other avenues in your life.

This scale can be an excellent starting place for you to think about your career development. The profile on the next page of this inventory will give you more specific information about your work importance. Read the scale descriptions on the next page and complete the exercises that are included in this scale. No matter how you scored, low, moderate or high, you will benefit from these exercises.

SECTION V: WORK-LEISURE BALANCE SCALE

Work-Leisure Balance Scale Descriptions

CAREER COMMITMENT

People scoring high on this scale are highly committed to the work role. They see work as a means to an end. Work meets and satisfies all of their needs. Work is the primary driving force in life. They tend to be motivated by external rewards at work. They tend to be result-orientated at work. They are willing and able to take on challenging projects. They tend to set realistic and attainable career goals.

WORK INVOLVEMENT

People scoring high on this scale are highly involved in the work role. They are willing to commit time, effort and energy needed to complete their work. They are motivated about their work and interested in learning about the company or organization for which they work. Their leisure time is often spent doing work-related tasks. They tend to be very productive during work hours.

PERSONALITY TYPE

People scoring high on this scale tend to have a "Type A" personality. They have a chronic sense of time urgency and feel they must accomplish something while at work and while at play. Their self-esteem is tied into their work. They feel guilty when they are not working. They tend to pressure themselves to achieve more in less time. They are very aggressive, ambitious and competitive.

TIME MANAGER

People scoring high on this scale tend to be time efficient. They are frugal with time. They feel like there is never enough time to complete necessary tasks. They believe that time should not be wasted. They are often impatient with the rate at which things occur. They desire to be successful in the shortest amount of time possible.

LEISURE STYLE

People scoring high on this scale view work as their leisure. They believe that their work is the greatest source of life satisfaction. Their leisure activities are always related to their work. They hardly engage in relaxing leisure activities. When they do engage in a leisure activity, they are very competitive. They feel uncomfortable when they are not working.

SECTION V: WORK-LEISURE BALANCE SCALE

Profile Interpretation for Summary of Work-Leisure Balance Scale

Everyone defines success in different ways. How each person defines success is based on what they value. Some people value work, some people value leisure and some value a combination of both as well as other things. To determine your SUMMARY, look at your Grand Total for your five scales on the scale and write it on the line below. Your score will range from 35 to 140.

MY GRAND TOTAL SCORE: _____

Interpreting Your Summary Score

Your summary is what you need and value and provides a picture of how you express your values. Circle below the orientation in which you scored highest:

TOTAL SCALES SCORES	TOTAL WORK-LEISURE BALANCE ORIENTATION SUMMARY
Scores from 35 to 55	Leisure Orientation
Scores from 56 to 76	Leisure-Work Orientation
Scores from 77 to 97	Balance Orientation
Scores from 98 to 118	Work-Leisure Orientation
Scores from 119 to 140	Workaholic Orientation

To help you learn more about your particular orientation, the following pages describe each of the orientations and then provides questions for you to answer that will help you to be successful.

(Go to the Profile Descriptions)

SECTION V: WORK-LEISURE BALANCE SCALE

Work-Leisure Balance Scale Orientation Summary Profile Descriptions
Leisure Orientation

Your leisure activities (family, friends, hobbies, community activities, etc.) are a great source of life satisfaction. You tend to engage in non-work activities in a compulsive manner. You would prefer it if you would not need to work at all. You only work because you feel obligated to do so. You tend to be spontaneous and playful, and do not experience much stress in your life. You tend to be non-competitive, are not driven and not ambitious to climb any corporate ladders. Your life is pushed by your feelings rather than drawn by goals. You are creative, and meaning in your life is derived from your leisure, family and relationships activities. Your rewards from your leisure are primarily intrinsic in nature. You tend to follow your impulses and inspirations so that your abilities and talents become realized. Your avoidance of work is as much a compulsion as overworking is for a workaholic. You can be too highly committed to leisure, that you are not even interested in work. If you do work you tend to be an unmotivated and unproductive employee. It may be beneficial for you to seek other types of work.

1. In what ways are you creative?

   _____

   _____

   _____

2. How can you ensure that the creative values in your life are not overwhelmed by the urgent need to work and make a living?

   _____

   _____

   _____

3. How can you turn your leisure interests into work? Can you get part-time or full-time work using your leisure interests? Can you start a small or home-based business using your leisure skills? Can you start a crafts and arts business?

   _____

   _____

SECTION V: WORK-LEISURE BALANCE SCALE

Work-Leisure Balance Scale Orientation Summary Profile Descriptions

Leisure-Work Orientation

You prefer other life activities rather than work or career. Working is viewed as a necessity to accomplish leisure, spend time with your family, or accomplish other life goals. For you, work or career is often viewed as a means to an end — leisure, etc. You become bored easily and are not committed to work. You are not interested in work that consume too much of your time and energy. You prefer to draw on your creativity rather than work toward achievements and career goals. You often look for and work at "traditional" work for a very short time and then quit to return to your many creative activities. You meet your needs for self-esteem and self-actualization through your hobbies, community activities and leisure experiences. You often do not have enough faith in your abilities and skills to aggressively pursue opportunities to make a living doing the creative things you enjoy. You could be prone to become discouraged and quit pursuing your dreams.

1. What are your favorite leisure activities?

_____

_____

_____

2. How do your leisure activities meet your needs for belonging and self-esteem?

_____

_____

_____

3. What is your primary dream?

_____

_____

_____

4. What steps do you need to take to reach your dream?

_____

_____

_____

SECTION V: WORK-LEISURE BALANCE SCALE

Work-Leisure Balance Scale Orientation Summary Profile Descriptions
Balanced Orientation

You enjoy working and will give your all at work. However, you need leisure to rejuvenate and express your creativity. You are able to meet your needs through a variety of work and leisure activities. You tend to be perfectly happy at work and at leisure. You enjoy a lifestyle comprised of a healthy mix of activities. You are well-balanced and very versatile. What you must guard against is allowing your work to be distracted by your leisure or letting your work take away from your leisure-time activities. You enjoy your work and your career but are not obsessed with it.

1. In your work, what are your aspirations and ambitions?
   _____
   _____

2. In your leisure time, how do you meet your needs?

   Companionship _____
   _____

   Self-esteem _____
   _____

   Self-actualization _____
   _____

   Creativity _____
   _____

3. At work, how do you meet your needs?

   Companionship _____
   _____

   Self-esteem _____
   _____

   Self-actualization _____
   _____

   Creativity _____
   _____

SECTION V: WORK-LEISURE BALANCE SCALE

Work-Leisure Balance Scale Orientation Summary Profile Descriptions

Work-Leisure Orientation

You work long hours and devote much energy to your work and your career. You prefer to work rather than participate in leisure activities or in activities with community, family and friends. You will perform well in demanding and challenging work. Leisure is somewhat important in your life, but only after all your work is completed. You are very results oriented and will often work extra hours to complete projects. You need work that is challenging to you and when you can set goals and timetables for your achievement. You can become obsessive because you are very determined to succeed. You appreciate recognition and will be persistent to get this recognition. You enjoy working under competitive pressures because one of your strengths is planning. You can be impatient with yourself and others working with and for you. Your thinking tends to be rigid and very logical and linear.

1. What types of work do you most enjoy doing?

   _____
   _____
   _____

2. How can you progress in your career (additional training, further education, taking on special projects at work, etc.)?

   _____
   _____
   _____

3. What are your leisure interests?

   _____
   _____
   _____

4. How do or how can your leisure activities help you in your career?

   _____
   _____
   _____

SECTION V: WORK-LEISURE BALANCE SCALE

Work-Leisure Balance Scale Orientation Summary Profile Descriptions
Workaholic Orientation

Your work is your greatest source of life satisfaction. Although there are leisure activities available to you, you prefer to work. You allocate most of your time and energy to the work role. You often feel guilty when you are not working. You are addicted to the work you do. You devote high levels of energy to completing your work assignments. You always get the work done even if you have to push others. You prize work and productivity to the exclusion of leisure and social activities. Although you produce work of very high standards, you are susceptible to work strain and burnout. You often are a perfectionist and thus you may have difficulties working with others. You are often hurried and relentless in meeting deadlines and can become obsessive and compulsive about work. You may even experience unpleasant withdrawal symptoms when not working.

1. How do you relax and manage your stress?

_____

_____

_____

2. When you do engage in leisure activities, what do you do?

_____

_____

_____

3. How can you find more time for leisure? What activities might be fun to explore?

_____

_____

_____

4. Are you over-committed? How can you reduce your workload?

_____

_____

_____

SECTION V: ACTIVITY HANDOUTS

Balancing Work and Leisure

Learning to balance work and leisure is a skill critical for occupational health and wellness. Workers in this information age are having an increasingly difficult time balancing work and leisure, in part because the pressures of work have intensified. Studies of workplace trends suggest that for many people the demands of work dominate life. This, in turn, has prompted claims that the quality of life, career satisfaction, life satisfaction, family dynamics and our sense of community are deteriorating.

Much of this pressure comes from the top down. Many corporate employers demand that employees work longer hours, take work home, work weekends and take less vacation time, forcing those employees to choose between work and leisure. In contrast, many new employees are calling for more balance between work and the rest of their lives. They don't want to provide unlimited and unconditional commitment to their work. In fact, recent research shows that many of the young adults entering the workforce are willing to sacrifice money for time, taking lower salaries in favor of more vacations or the ability to work from home.

What needs do you have that are not being met by your work?

_____

_____

_____

How do your leisure activities fulfill your needs?

_____

_____

_____

How can you find more time for leisure?

_____

_____

_____

What new leisure activities would you explore if you had more time?

_____

_____

(Continued on the next page)

Balancing Work and Leisure *(Continued)*

In addition to simply choosing and engaging in your favorite leisure activities, there are other things you can do to have a more balanced career and life. Consider the following as you seek to find your balance.

Time for relationships — It is important that you take time each day to connect with important people in your life. This may mean scheduling this time (actually writing it in a calendar or planner) until you begin to adopt it as a permanent part of your day.

Time alone — Take time for yourself. Use it to reflect and recharge. Try meditating each day. Meditation can help you focus on the moment and stop thinking about work that needs to be done in the future.

Breaks — You can easily build breaks into your work schedule. Even if you have been working quite well without taking breaks, you probably have not experienced your optimum level of creativity, motivation and energy. Almost all employers allow for some breaks during the day. If not, request break-time.

Exercise — Exercise has been shown to be an excellent stress buster. People who exercise regularly tend to be happier, are more energetic, have a better outlook on life and are able to cope much more effectively with stress. A short walk at lunch time or up and down stairs is better than none at all.

Vacations — Use your vacation time for rest and relaxation. Everyone has a different idea about what constitutes rest and relaxation. Some people like vacations with sight-seeing. Others prefer to rent a cabin on the lake. The secret is to commit to using your vacation days (don't try to carry them over without a great reason for doing so) and finding a restful way to spend them.

SECTION V: JOURNALING ACTIVITIES

Workaholism or Not?

Why do you feel the need to work so much or so little?

___

Why type of work-leisure balance did you experience in your family growing up?

___

My Work

What do you like most about the work you do or have done in the past?

_____
_____
_____
_____
_____
_____
_____
_____
_____
_____

What do you like least about the work you do or have done in the past?

_____
_____
_____
_____
_____
_____
_____
_____
_____
_____

Finding Your Balance Between Work and Leisure

For peak performance on the job — and to avoid being a workaholic . . .

- Work regular hours and take work home only when absolutely necessary

- Engage in a variety of activities outside of work

- Select hobbies that are different from the work you do everyday

- Feel comfortable delegating work to others

- Find time to relax on the weekends

- Develop friendships outside of the workplace

- Talk about things other than work

- Avoid being identified by the work you do

- Develop connections outside of work – find comfortable spaces related to community and spirituality

- Build rejuvenating breaks into your work schedule

- Look at vacations as a time to relax and reconnect with yourself, family and/or friends – leave your electronic devices at home!

Why Leisure Matters

LEISURE ENHANCES YOUR WORK/LIFE BALANCE THROUGH THESE ASPECTS:

- an increased sense of freedom
- companionship and relationships with others
- creativity and self-expression
- development of interpersonal and social skills
- enhancement of character and personality
- entertainment
- feeling of independence
- physical health and variety in life
- relaxation
- self-fulfillment and personal meaning
- self-improvement and self-definition
- vocational exploration

Whole Person Associates is the leading publisher of training resources for professionals who empower people to create and maintain healthy lifestyles. Our creative resources will help you work effectively with your clients in the areas of stress management, wellness promotion, mental health and life skills.

Please visit us at our web site: **WholePerson.com**. You can check out our entire line of products, place an order, request our print catalog, and sign up for our monthly special notifications.

Whole Person Associates

800-247-6789